my itty-bitty bio

Albert Einstein

Published in the United States of America by Cherry Lake Publishing
Ann Arbor, Michigan
www.cherrylakepublishing.com

Content Adviser: Ryan Emery Hughes, Doctoral Student, School of Education, University of Michigan
Reading Adviser: Marla Conn MS, Ed., Literacy specialist, Read-Ability, Inc.
Book Design: Jennifer Wahl
Illustrator: Jeff Bane

Photo Credits: ©Mapics/Shutterstock, 5; ©Brian Goodman/Shutterstock, 7; ©Twin Design/Shutterstock, 9; ©Photodiem/Shutterstock, 11; ©Everett Historical/Shutterstock, 13; ©retoncy/Shutterstock, 15, 22; ©Everett Historical/Shutterstock, 17; ©Sueddeutsche Zeitung Photo / Alamy Stock Photo, 19, 23; ©PD-US-not renewed John D. Schliff, 21; Cover, 6, 8, 14, Jeff Bane; Various frames throughout, ©Shutterstock Images

Library of Congress Cataloging-in-Publication Data

Names: Devera, Czeena, author.
Title: Albert Einstein / by Czeena Devera.
Other titles: My itty-bitty bio.
Description: Ann Arbor : Cherry Lake Publishing, [2018] | Series: My itty-bitty bio | Audience: K to grade 3. | Includes bibliographical references and index.
Identifiers: LCCN 2018003695| ISBN 9781534128866 (hardcover) | ISBN 9781534132061 (pbk.) | ISBN 9781534130562 (pdf) | ISBN 9781534133761 (hosted ebook)
Subjects: LCSH: Einstein, Albert, 1879-1955--Juvenile literature. | Physicists--Biography--Juvenile literature.
Classification: LCC QC16.E5 D48 2018 | DDC 530.092 [B] --dc23
LC record available at https://lccn.loc.gov/2018003695

Printed in the United States of America
Corporate Graphics

table of contents

About the author: Czeena Devera grew up in the red-hot heat of Arizona surrounded by books. Her childhood bedroom had built-in bookshelves that were always too full. She now lives in Michigan with an even bigger library of books.

About the illustrator: Jeff Bane and his two business partners own a studio along the American River in Folsom, California, home of the 1849 Gold Rush. When Jeff's not sketching or illustrating for clients, he's either swimming or kayaking in the river to relax.

I grew up around smart people. My father and uncle were **engineers**.

I went to college in Switzerland. I studied to be a teacher. But I couldn't find a job.

What jobs do your parents have?

Instead, I worked at an office. I wrote over 300 papers in my free time. They were about **physics**.

I became famous for my ideas. My work led to the **atomic bomb** being made. I didn't help build it. I didn't like war.

I won the **Nobel Prize**.
I changed how people studied math and science.

What would you like to change?

I died in 1955. I loved sharing what I learned. My discoveries helped shape today's world.

What would you like to ask me?

timeline

1901

1870

Born
1879

1921

1970

Died
1955

glossary

atomic bomb (uh-TAH-mik BAHM) a very powerful bomb that explodes with great force, heat, and bright light

compass (KUHM-puhs) an instrument with a magnetic needle that always points north; used for finding directions

engineers (en-juh-NEERZ) people who are specially trained to design and build machines or large structures such as bridges and roads

Nobel Prize (noh-BEHL PRIZE) an award that encourages people to work hard in fields that help all people; it is given out every year

physics (FIZ-iks) the study of movement, force, light, heat, sound, and electricity

index